F U R I E S

A P O E T R Y A N T H O L O G Y
O F W O M E N W A R R I O R S

EDITED BY
EVE LACEY

All profits from this anthology will be divided equally between both
For Books' Sake and Rape Crisis England & Wales, supporting
women writers and survivors of rape and sexual violence.

First published in 2014 by
Group Of
on behalf of
For Books' Sake
www.forbookssake.net
This paperback edition published 2015

A CIP catalogue record for this book is available from the British Library.

ISBN: 978-0-956665-16-4

Printed in EU by Pulsio SARL

CONTENTS

FOREWORD

Furies are the daughters of Gaia, female spirits of justice and vengeance, and these poets are all of those things and more. They are Joan of Arc and Bonnie Parker slinging shots in a backstreet bar; they are poets who care not whether they are damned or see with the eyes of angels, only that there is the word and there is death and in between the sound of someone scribbling their words at dawn, or looking out of their window to see someone else's words written across the morning sky.

In this anthology, women are womb carriers, crows, hair plaiters, fornicators; the Lord is asked to stop them climbing mountains for fear of what exactly they might see, their touch is firmer than a man's, they hurdle the amber moon by accident, rise with November's detritus and find a hint of flame in the morning sky. They are swans and selkies, they are bone, they are sky, they dream by fires enclosed by wired fences, they plunge their heads deep underwater, migrate to the blank page of the tundra. Secrets are hunted snakes on silver leashes, a mother's warm gun still smokes by the door. Detect the presence of enemies: Betty Draper shoots at her neighbour's pigeons, and she's smoking the whole time. A grandmother ingrains in her daughters exactly that they should never have to endure violence against them, how hard they must be, how little they can tolerate.

In these poems there is blood, there is rape and there are women strong in heart and soul no matter what they've walked through in this life or the next, women who open up their chest and let you see within. There is fury, there is recognition, these poems know each other, they have met before, seen each other's symbols, heard stories and never bowed their head or looked the other way. It is hard to talk about rape — this is a line that the others nod to and each of these poems does so with beauty, grace, fearlessness: unencumbered by a need to please or acquiesce, to dilute or deny. Rape is used as a tool of war; it is in every town, city, village. There is always a footstep in the street, a corner to turn, a husband to face, a brother, a stranger. Until every woman, man and child in this world is safe, we must continue to raise our voices louder, to let no stone go unwritten on.

To be voiceless is to question whether one even exists — so listen to these voices — for all of those who cannot speak out and for all those who are waiting to hear these words and know them as their own; to all those who understand that rape is a war we must all continue to challenge and fight in every country, every day, from now until the human race finally, truly, evolves. Until then — let it be known that we stood side-by-side on the long road home, and said, enough is enough.

Jenni Fagan
Edinburgh, 2014

INTRODUCTION

'There must be those among whom we can sit down and weep,
and still be counted as warriors.'
Adrienne Rich, *Sources*

'Dear Antigone, I take it as the task of the translator to forbid
you should ever lose your screams.'
Anne Carson, *Antigonick*

We embarked on *Furies* in the hope of re-writing women warriors. Part of this mission would entail recalling their prowess, but the more important aspect would be to challenge the definition. Adrienne Rich and Anne Carson would guide us in this quest — we wanted to reconfigure the notion of warrior, broaden its bounds through time and vulnerability, and still retain the scream.

The call for submissions brought more Furies than I had dreamt possible. The theme was interpreted widely and wildly, and I was struck by the solidarity in every poem. Each rewrote another aspect of womanhood, and every one succeeded in our aim: to take a sinner and spin her anew. This anthology holds the very best of over 700 entries from around the world. It is divided into six sections: *Shoal, Garden, Feral, Entrails, Myth* and *Resurrection*.

We begin with a voyage, and Isabel Rogers sets sail with a de-barnacled boat. This ship goes forth loosed from anchors and rigging, and as the way progresses, the weather turns tempestuous, and vengeance wreaks the full ocean havoc of Emily Blewitt's 'Wrecker'.

Shoal is where the tides will turn and where the stories of old undergo a sea-change. In tribute to Adrienne Rich's weeping warriors, the subjects of these verses both wave and drown, sink and swim. The sea is a place of wreckage and leaks, where voyages are wrought and ruined, but the warriors of *Shoal* resurface for the length of a poem to issue their stories like spindrift into the night. These poems are filled with fish and birds, they establish the first inklings of animal defiance. It seems that rewriting requires a metamorphosis, and vengeance is best pictured in beasts.

Etymologically speaking, 'anthology' means gathered flowers. The flora of our *Garden* section is not for ornament but for growth, and *Furies* embraces the weeds. From mountaineers with an improper interest in the outdoors, to wicked witchery in the swamps, green can be the colour of feminist protest and the garden requires a woman's fight to save its song.

Garden rewrites the feminine body of land: these grounds will not be conquered, rather the poets envision a new topography as they hike and burn and leap. For every wrong there is a botanic cure, because the earth cannot help but regenerate, and just as Helen Mort's climbers will 'pull on the initials of the dead', so our Furies pen a new lay of the land.

Feral looks to the fauna of that habitat. The Furies take many forms: swan, rabbit, peacock and wolf. Mostly though, they do not settle for one disguise. They are chimeric, and there is an element of rogue taxidermy to their disarray. As in *Shoal*, the *Feral* works as a mode of becoming and, from Susan Richardson's 'wing-cloak' to Angela Readman's 'swanskin', the transition from wronged woman to avenger requires a furry pelt. Our Furies don animal masks to tackle the harder tasks: this is a menagerie of both the hunted and their prey, and some things can only be articulated through the zoo.

Entrails deals with the gore. Reconfiguring can be bloody, and will almost always leave scars. It is especially visceral in fantasy, when writers use words to topple fear and turn the threat back round on itself. Poetry is a safe space to play with danger, and butchery is the imagining of the dispossessed. This most basic of vengeance leaves behind human remains, but a body makes for an excellent story to those who know how to read it. Our poets vivisect that carnal tale.

Each punishment subjects the crime to a form of poetic justice: Circe's men are made pig, Rhea will eat Cronus and retrieve her children from his gut. Cruelty bleeds into the landscape; Jodie Ashdown's 'eviscerated stomach lies as poppies on the ground', and colour splashes from human to animal to floor in poems rendered so powerfully that you can taste the lick of blood on teeth.

Myth is the section that perhaps most directly addresses our theme. In *Furies*, myth is unbound from the 'fatherbrotheruncleson' of history in Imtiaz Dharker's verse, and lost into new word orders. Kassandra finds herself back on trend in hashtag resurrection. The prophets of the modern age dispel their auguries in no more than 140 characters, but Vahni Capildeo calls for pause and a more careful reading than the scroll of the internet browser.

These women are oneiric, so wrought with centuries' significance that they have become shorthand for murder, or loss, or tragedy. Their stories have spilt the bounds of just one body and they find themselves peopled with many versions of a woman.

For some, the strain of time is palpable and occupying the cultural imagination for millennia begins to take its toll — Kiran Millwood Hargrave's 'Medusa' sees time roll by like rocks: 'Most days though, follow on. It's a case of taking them, one by one.' One by one then, these retellings join the ranks of so many before, and contribute to the longevity of their myths. But *Furies* positions mythic women as more than just easy symbols — they are storytellers, and architects of their own malingering tales. These poems are invitations to imagine them otherwise, to examine what traits warrant such obstinate survival, and to ask what proves muse to so many for so long. The answer lies somewhere in the cross section of gods and prayer, flight and fancy. Or, as Kalliope Amorphous puts it, 'at the vanishing point of chariot and church.'

Resurrection is for those poems that come ghosting into our midst, and in memory of the women who continue to haunt history at its margins. It entails a word of warning — misogyny kills, but writing may resurrect the long-dead. These poems take place in the edgeland between life and death; they revive old tales with lines that are condensed into rhyme and cut to the quick.

Some figures have been reincarnated so many times that they are no longer recognisable as their original. Therein lies the freedom of repetition, which uses small distortions, many times made, to loose a character from the author and allow them to take on a life of their own. We realise that the first story was as much a fantasy as our own, and that the truth can change every time we tell it.

Anna Kisby touches on the importance of the archive to this mission. Conservation is the largest part of resurrection: every phoenix needs some ashes from which to rise. This collection stands as record to those embers, a catalogue of heroines that will use the archive to buffer death. Fragments and objects survive, dust refuses to settle. Poetry is an act of transubstantiation and museums provide the prompt. For such recent rebels as the suffragettes, there are still remnants, relics and dust, and every time we inhale their bodies, we exhume their soul.

Resurrection can be lonely. A Lazarus trick is often obliged to revisit some horror, for the last memory is rarely the best. Several poems take place in a court of justice, where *Furies* arise to set the story straight once and for all. For many, the trick spans only the space of a verse in which they tell their tale. The rest of the resurrection, the living on beyond the page, relies on the reader to keep retelling and retelling, and then telling once more. Our best gift is to follow Malika Booker's advice and bear witness, 'so death no lick we down tonight.'

We begin with a ship and end with ghosts: *Furies* is a haunting, a tempest and a scream. Claire Askew's title and neologism, 'Poltergeistrix,' comes to stand for all the resurrected: traditionally, ghosts haunt because they still have something left to tell. This is their stage.

Eve Lacey
Cambridge, 2014

PART 1

SHOAL

The Voyage

She is set fair.
No more will storms
buffet and tug.
Her anchor weighed,

she swallowed link
on lumpen link,
and bit down hard:
watched it sink alone

with grim delight.
Her sails fill.
Safe through rocks
toward the sunset

and the deep wide sea
of fable and her memory.
No more tickling crew,
forever rearranging

her rigging. De-barnacled
in port, now sleek
under the waterline,
she flexes her rudder,

oiled supple, and executes
a perfect figure of eight.
Dolphins sew
her bow seam straight.

Any moment
she will shake loose
the crow's nest,
lean her mast

into full weather,
conjure new sap
from brine and algae;
encourage leaves.

Isabel Rogers

Nerrivik

Do not mistake me for a mermaid.
Do not presume I'll swim to the surface,
perch on a berg and croon.
Do not tell your kids coddled in caribou fur
a fairytale of my creation.
Hold the kayak of truth to their ears:
let them hear
        the slice
of the knife when my father chopped
        off my fingers,
my arctic howl as I sank
                to the ocean floor,
the bloodsong of my thumbs as they bulged
        with blubber —
before my icestruck eyes, belugas formed.
My index fingers were instant narwhals —
                tusks burst
from nails. Ringed seals zinged
        from my middle fingers, while the littlest wriggled
far from mammaldom, riddled with gills and scales.

Do not, however, spear me with pity.
If my whalejaw comb cracks,
if the stumps of my wrists can't clear
the knots from the thick black fronds of my hair,
I can summon a shaman to tackle the tangles,
with the weave and tickle of mackerel and cod.

All I demand is that you treat this zone,
which I was forced to make my home, with care.
Do not thaw my ceiling.
Do not stain my walls with your crimson greed.
Don't rip up my floor with your trawlers.
Don't furnish me with debris from your submarines.

Remember — one shrug   of my shoulders can cause
a four-day storm. I can calve bergs
                                        from glaciers
with the smallest sneeze. If I am displeased,
I will call the offspring of my fingers to me
and make fists to breach   your overwater world,
                    to punch
              your beloved sun   from its   sky.

Susan Richardson

Fishing, I Lose Another

Because you left me in Ketchikan
I taught myself to catch the cutthroat,

standing creek-like, tapered trap of my hands
motionless to the point of no sensation.

I slept on a cushion of air
between the bear cub and its mother,

ate berries that stained
my fingers the shade of your veins.

I ran beside the Douglas squirrel
from hollow to sky and back,

bathed in a duff of needles
gathered beneath another's limbs.

I bear-walked the trail with elderberry and fern
arboring the shape of my spine,

braided cat's tail moss into my hair.
I stood shouldered between firs to watch you pass,

chose not to say your name
to prevent its lodging like a fishbone in my throat.

Jenifer Browne Lawrence

The Sister Next to Be Born

Isn't she the one who's prone to falling
from the clothesline, strand of hair sucked
to sable brush tip between her teeth?
The one we tracked from Little Chief smoker
to roadside shoulder pocketing coins of highway
drunks who palmed her sockeyes on the slope
below the snow, river long past melt, the sky strung
with milky lies we told at night — in our folded hands
the stolen smoke, kitchen match a siren call
across her zipper, flame like sunlight and the cheap
inhale out the door while father slept between
Zane Grey and Rainier. We woke him once to view
a purple ridge along her cheekbone. In drying time
the clothespin tries to mind her fish-quick tongue.

Jenifer Browne Lawrence

Tsunami Sale

In August the Lemon Creek Glacier breathes
turpitude and silt. It drips, abacus
of present worth, counting days I loved
the potato-faced fisherman whose hands
held me like a net, who sailed to Dutch
Harbor and set his anchor there. I heard
he married Arbutus, a woman who,
men say, eats salmon hearts to flush her breast
with fire. I suppose the clutter comes
with the house, doublewide tabernacle
I am never going to sell. The tide passes
through. I hear it come — igneous shift,
sovereign rumble of another quake,
and plant my legs as though I am at sea.

Jenifer Browne Lawrence

Pwll y Wrach

Yes, I confess I was ejected
from those woods where I spelled
girls into deer and men into bears,
and yes, I veered west, hurdled one sea,
then wester yet to this opposite
                of woods,
where kittiwakes crest knucklebone crags
and heckle the land-bound.

See those cliffs? They're not Ordovician.
All the buckles
                and rucks, the rifts
and the folds, are mine.
I shoulder-shunted   the sandstones and shales,
licked out that cwm,
filled it with spit, then blasted
a pit with just one exhale,
where lichen and froth, shingle and salt,
can mingle. No, it's not geological,
this place where I still aim to save
the frustrated from their fate.

Take you, for instance.
I can smell that you're walking to escape —
yet you could go so much further
than the path's death at Amroth.
Come. Don't let your resolve flit
from squill to thrift like a Burnet moth.
My draughts are seasonal —
today, I give you stitchwort and sheepsbit.
Drink, and they'll trigger a shift
into guillemot or shag — seabirds are my specialty —
while two moons on,
swigging knapweed and betony will release you
                into seal.
You could even join my coven of slugs,
each one fat as a capstone.

I also offer unction.
Dump your rucksack. Roll your shoulders.
Feel me rub forth
                a choughful of wings.

Susan Richardson

Selkie Wife Letter

Some nights,
when my new limbs
are caught in his
and coarse blankets,
I hear you,

my blubbery kin
echoing
across the sound
ochone ochone ...

I'm lairing here,
a netted animal,
greeting brine,
a mumping seal.

The cast of his body,
the thief of me,
is salt-cracked
branches, lichens

and I am forbidden
to follow his trawling.
He likes my canine eyes
I hide my jaggy teeth.

Often I hear squalling.
Today I was trying
to card wool, itching
to kelp dive,

like you, the reeling finfeet.
These legs aren't used
to being legs so long.
The wind gives me vertigo.

I'm always looking
for my skin,
sea-coloured, iridescent.
Today: more skelloching,

smashed pots,
fish guts smeared
on the floor. A shimmer.
I am a monstrous mother.

Francine Elena

To Sing as Legends Do

After Sylvia Plath's 'Lorelei'

i.

I leave this
for you to find
now, when the bleached sun
blinds you, where
pockmarked limestone
touches the river:

a cold body,
hollow as bird's-wing bones,

echoing, skin and hair
a thin collection of salt,
spilled, tossed along
the gaping shore

which cradles this body
like algae and cigarette butts.

ii.

Listen for me there,
where the current caught
my last elegy.

Know me for my spine,
my wide fish eyes,
my unhooked mouth;

but do not hope for touch —
you'll not own
this deserted, flooded
howl, death-dealing
whisper, which lingers

here, in this wild,
unblessed churchyard.

Nic Campeotto

Wrecker

For you, I'll light beacons.
Wait for my signal —

I'll beckon you in.
Will you come to me

smiling, lightly recall
that we've been here before;

walked, hand in hand,
clutching our shoes?

Come. Here,
I'll take you

freighted with silk,
eyes round like coins.

I'll strike from your finger
the ring that she gave you;

watch while you flounder,
waves rise to claim you.

Boy, when you drown
no soul shall save you.

Emily Blewitt

PART 2

GARDEN

Litany

Oh woman you rockstone.
Oh woman you hairy bank.
Oh woman you invisible.
Oh woman hands always akimbo.
Oh woman you downtrodden grass.
Oh woman you disposable pillar of salt.
Oh woman you sacrificed land.
Oh woman you womb carrier.
Oh woman you crow.
Oh woman you infertile.
Oh woman you baby maker.
Oh woman you single woman
Oh woman you child rearer.
Oh woman you lowly snake.
Oh woman you sand pit.
Oh woman you non-begater.
Oh woman you bleeder
Oh woman you pleasurer.
Oh woman you sister.
Oh woman you friend.
Oh woman you whore.
Oh woman you wife.
Oh woman you unworthy of being a disciple.
Oh woman you pile of salt.
Oh woman you easily dash-away-able.
Oh woman only marriage-able.
Oh woman easily unmentionable.
Oh woman bitter fruit
Oh woman sister deceiver.
Oh woman easily invisible.
Oh woman you hair plaiter.
Oh woman fornicator.
Oh woman feet washer
Oh woman.

Malika Booker

Lord, Stop Her Climbing Mountains

Letter from Elizabeth Le Blond's aunt, c.1909

Lord, stop her climbing mountains.
She has scandalised all London.
Lord, she looks like a Red Indian.
Her naked arms, uncovered knee…

God, stop her climbing mountains.
The air has seen enough of her.
Her touch is firmer than a man's.
Her fingers move improperly.

Lord, stop her climbing mountains.
A view should not unfold like that
without a window keeping it.
I am afraid of what she'll see.

Helen Mort

Height

Fanny Bullock Workman jumps a crevasse above the Hispar, Karakorum.

I hated that leap,
by matchless dark,
across four feet, invisible.

It was only
a bed's width, only
an arm span, less than my height.

I seemed so light
I might not land again;
go clear above the seracs

and the frozen scarps,
hopscotch the stars, hurdle
the amber moon by accident.

Just for a breath, I flew,
afraid you could not anchor me,
the earth not bring me back.

Helen Mort

Above Cromford

for Alison Hargreaves

Your body tight against the cold
inside a tent high on K2

you dream about Black Rocks:
squat monoliths, tattooed with names,

routes so graffitied
that you'd sink your fingers

into letters, pull
on the initials of the dead.

You didn't need to carve your own.
Your signature was grip and lift,

partnerless dance that
left no mark, and as you moved

the sequences spelled out
your name. And it was

unrepeatable. And gone
when you looked back.

Helen Mort

On Mending

Outside
the mistle thrush sits tall on his perch
and rehearses his song in dread of the fieldfares
that raid the garden's dwindling stores.

Inside the white room
she accepts a bunch of unseasonal flowers;
he stands with his thumb down a pinstripe seam

and when he's gone
she pounds her fists until the grout clogs with red
and she's hoisted by her armpits, slung on the bed

where she watches them at work,
in Technicolor, across her lids,
sprinkling salt in his tea,
cutting paper dolls
in the folds of The Times.

Outside
heronries nest as many as ten pairs
while a fluffed teal splashes
and a shelduck tosses his emerald head.

Inside the white room
she accepts a bunch of unseasonal flowers;
he stands with his thumb down a pinstripe seam

and when he's gone
she pounds her fists until the grout clogs with red
and she's hoisted by her armpits, slung on the bed

where she watches them at work,
in Technicolor, across her lids,
pinching his doughy
calves until he cramps
under Irish linen sheets.

Outside
leaves mesh green through brown moss
and hazel catkins expand;
snowdrops shine.

Inside the white room
she accepts a bunch of unseasonal flowers;
he stands with his thumb down a pinstripe seam

and when he's gone

Jo Dixon

Dear Jenny

Dear Jenny Greenteeth,
Underneath the mire,
Cackling ever silently,
With eyes as red as fire.
Look at how your fingers
Glisten in the night,
Slippery, polished red,
My Jenny's hellish light.

Aren't you ever lonely
In the clammy gloom?
Your hands grasp theirs
In hungry pain desperate to consume
You line the bloated bodies up
Their skin as white as chalk
They're pretty dollies, dearie,
But dead men cannot talk.

Oh Jenny, can't I join you?
And help you scream and howl?
Can't I rage and tear and rip?
Can't I prowl as you do prowl?
I might be weak and small,
But there is hunger in me too,
We both share the longing,
Why is the eating just for you?

Jenny, won't you help me?
I can't jump in on my own,
Everyone is watching
And I feel it in my bones,
Please drag me to the marsh,
And protect me from their stares,
I will suffocate on land,
There's only hunger for me there.

Ailie Kerr

Greenham Common, 1985

Everything is monochrome, but for the fire
which she feeds and coaxes like a child,
they can't help but see it, the men behind the wire

who keep guard all year, as if she were a thing gone wild,
which she supposes she is to certain minds
who don't take trouble with, but interrogate this mild

and gentle figure. She is only fending off the cold, inclined
to nothing stronger than a rebel song, a mug of tea,
yet her daughter has forsaken her, to which she is resigned —

principle was never a wedding guest with suitable repartee.
Now anything so formal has no meaning,
there is only this camp, the stolen heath, the wind in the trees,

and the men behind the wire watching
this woman beside a fire dreaming.

Julie-ann Rowell

Gaia's Autumn

She rises with November's detritus:
bonfires settling into their remains
and the hint of flame in the morning sky
is reflected in her grate. She has coaxed
the range awake and light warms the parchment-
skin of her cheeks, appled against
the notched spine of a post,
softened by age and woodworm.

Her hip is crumbling and her hands are arthritic
knots — all eight decades have gnarled them
into paws that dance around their clumsiness,
plucking rosemary needles with a deftness
that belies such heaviness of limb
and defectiveness of finger. She folds and rolls,
tucks and smooths as her pie grows. The ruffled edge
of a cigarette hangs from her bottom lip —
it has formed a catkin of ash, poised
to float from her mouth, grey and silent
as only the breath of her words might fall
to filter through the morning, like sunlight
seeking the floor through angled window slats.

Gaia dreams in the chatter of a young girl's mouth
as a word-crumb dissolves on the tip of her tongue.

Elisabeth Sennitt Clough

PART 3

FERAL

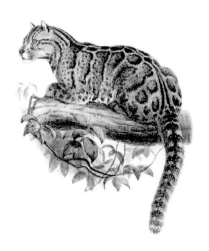

Peacock

Never mind the pea hen who screams
from the green grass, shedding brown

whilst in the garden he casts a blue shadow
and she squats behind the topiary, waited.

I wail and trample my eggs
and leave my wet nest stinking.

Rebecca White

The Pen is Mightier

What seemed like a lover's tongue between my toes
was the forming of extra skin.
What my spine believed were prickles of unease
were the birth-hurts of feathers.
The words I found to shout and curse
hardened into a beak,
while the flex of my stretched neck almost choked me.

So now you've got the daughter you desired.
Bride-white. Pond-perfect.
And, aside from this ridiculous hiss,
no ability to vocalise.

But listen, mother —
when I appear to be gliding
or serenely preening, I will shrug
your fluffed-up gloats off my back
and plunge my head
                           deep underwater.
I will see what you don't see, tease out
the tangles in the sub-aquatic weeds.

And when I emerge,
I'll learn to run on the surface, unfold
              my wing-cloak,
                           rise.

Watch me migrate
to the blank page of the tundra,
fill my bill with indelible sky and begin

to write.

Susan Richardson

Featherweight

The farrier hands me a stone like an egg,
heart shaped enough. I carry it, laden with love.

We'll marry on a Monday in a church that costs less.
I will wear a plain shift, loaded with only one
shade of white, rivers ironed off my back.

Outside the woodshed Mother bites the webs
of her hands to black scabs. I nod, speak only hisses.
Our eyes are varnish, keep what we won't say intact.

She lights the swanskin. It burns like a sigh.
The air plucks smoky strands, wisps dust the dusk.

Forever, the skin felt so big, hand-me-down feathers
too heavy for flight. Then it fit like a blizzard, down
between my legs clawed my petticoat to bits, swept

up my skinny legs. It was the same for her, I suppose
— this flying and loving and not knowing how to stop.
The steel of our wings can break first love's back

— we do not know our span. Boys who got too close
to the sunset balanced on my beak snapped, spines
like reeds whistling at the wind. The skin spits.

Mother pokes the ash, her neck is a coat hook
hanging up the moonlight. I, too, will marry
a solid man who never saw me as a swan.

He will not know as birds we miss nothing, yet
when he kisses me, softly, woman, I miss my beak.

Angela Readman

Lida and the Swan

He was a master of the hunt, whom nobody and nothing could escape.
— film star Lida Baarova on her lover, Joseph Goebbels

He does not swoop. He drags
his webbed foot across the carpet,
taller in his dress uniform.

Still, he speaks and my back arches.
And at first it feels like mating:
we are gliding in what must be water,

out past barricades and boats;
his narrow lips peck my neck,
his strange heart flaps against my breast.

Until my sheets crackle with wiretap-static,
the black limousine circles the block
even after he's left.

Until he thrusts his tongue down my throat
and I taste blacklist, newsprint;
inhale gasoline and flesh.

Tonight, he will come, moulting khaki,
clumsy with fruits and chocolates.
I will be in the scarlet peignoir, ready,

drumming lacquered nails against
my loosening thighs — see, darling?
my own scalpels: red-mooned, ready.

Shelley Puhak

After Another Friend Told Me She Was Sexually Assaulted

Secrets are snakes. Biting constantly
When stepped on, painful, and hard
To put back in cages.
Memories are silver. Shiny or dull
Depending upon whose they are.
Being a girl can be a hunted animal
On a dirt road filled with holes,
Surrounded by mirrors it
Knows are never clear;
Is told are never clear, repeatedly,
Yet still feels shocked
When things appear more distorted
Than it feels it was led to believe they will be.
Being a woman is the same thing
Except the holes,
Because unlike girls
Women are not supposed to fall into them.
These secrets that we hold
Are hunted snakes on silver leashes,
Venom restrained only by memory,
Attached to what is chasing them,
Slithering down dirt roads filled with holes,
Surrounded by mirrors
That constantly tell them where to go;
The wrong way, and
They know it's the wrong way,
They've been shown it's the wrong way,
They've been told that this, this is
The wrong way,
Yet go there anyway to escape.

It is easier to fall into potholes on the road
Than it is to climb into a cage.

It is hard to talk about rape.

Bridget Minamore

A Daughter Sings From the Earth

My mother shoots birds for their feathers,
sometimes crows for their size and their sheen.

She'll crouch by the lake in all weathers
to bring down the right shade of green.

I arrive home from school; it is teatime.
Her warm gun still smokes by the door.

I find her hunched over her pluckings
while my sister sweeps birds off the floor.

As daughters, we both have our duties,
but Icarus, a boy, has got none.

Whatever he does, can't be faulted.
Neighbours say: A highflyer, that son.

My Dad spends all day in his workshop.
Nearly finished, he whistles and sings.

I can guess what he's making. But I ask this:
Why does Icarus, my brother, need wings?

Diana Brodie

She-wolf

It starts as a reflexive flinch
from smells previously tolerated —

the burn of bleach, tobacco's sickly cinders,
wine's sour gastric fumes —

while others offer solace: roasting meat,
untainted air, my husband's skin.

He is intrigued by my shifting expression
as I process the approach of food, wince

at the metallic slap of the waiter's sweat.
I relish this new sense, resolve to keep it.

It enables me to know my friends,
detect the presence of enemies.

Suzanna Fitzpatrick

Bunny Girl

The Cadbury's Caramel Bunny
has large enchanting eyes,
a smile as smooth as honey
and taut but tender thighs

melting from her mini-dress
like tempting chocolate fingers,
while quivering marshmallow breasts
invite the gaze to linger.

Such perfect femininity:
unthreatening, seductive;
sex sells, even confectionery,
with women most productive.

So let's aspire to slender waists,
huge boobs and tiny noses;
conform each figure, every face
to coy — but sexy — poses,

just like our poster girl, who should
be blushing as she smoulders;
bearing ideal womanhood
on rabbit's furry shoulders.

Suzanna Fitzpatrick

Betty Draper Shoots At Her Neighbour's Pigeons

Gone noon, in ivory nightgown,
one Lucky Strike jutting
from her mouth, she tips up the gun

and aims at their swooping grace.
The crack that comes
rouses the man who threatened

her children's dog, his remaining birds
now panicked in their cage.
She keeps firing, sheer sleeves

slipping to her elbows, and maybe
there's a shot in there for her husband Don,
his absences at night.

Maybe a shot for motherhood too,
and the era that keeps her
like a butterfly, pinned in the home

with her rioting young. The hours
of dishes, laundry, all of it accomplished
with that silent, divine face.

On a perfect lawn, glossed nails
on the trigger, Betty Draper
shoots at her neighbour's pigeons

and she's smoking the whole time.

Rebecca Goss

37

PART 4

ENTRAILS

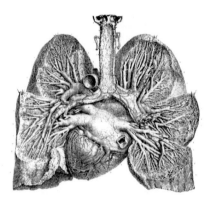

Warning

1

Some great grandmother told her daughter,
never let no man hit you and sleep,
pepper the food, boil hot water and throw,
use knife and make clean cut down there,
use cutlass and chop, then go police.
Each daughter told over and over,
like *brush your teeth,* till it stick.
How my mother run-way man with cutlass,
chase him. How my gran use cutlass pon table
to explain to her man, *Don't lose your blasted mind*
and raise that hand on me.
And so we are shaped, moulded and made hard.
I remember my aunt kicked her man out
after her child was born, cut him dead
like rotten wood, after he use her like boxing bag,
kicking her womb as she lay on the floor.
That day her blood boiled through swell eye
and buss skin. She knew he could not sleep; he knew
she wanted to kill him bad bad, chop him dead…

2

Raised in London soil and Guyana sun,
I never understood that need for cutlass,
where it came from, till I visited Grenada,
a place where man fist pound woman flesh
like kneading hard dough. I see bull strength
knock girls flat out when she man full of rum
and carnival. How Ronald buss lash in he woman ass
every Friday and Saturday night, kick she down,
buss she tail. And next day is black eye and bruise.
As Pauline clings onto Ronald's foot, saying
She love him through each blow, I understand.

3

I never knew I had it. Thought I was soft,
till that night my friend could not drive
and I offered him my bed to sleep,
I felt something in his look, he and I
alone in that room, and my blood raised up.
my pores swelled, I went to the kitchen,
took down that knife, marched upstairs,
told him, *I cutting it off if you lose your mind.*
Don't think it and if you do, don't sleep.

Malika Booker

Circe

Daily I watch my men.

Their suffering is
carefully curated —
a pinkening for each time
they denied me,

a trotter for each time
they forced me,
and finally —
that tassel of a tail.

I end the day with a meal,
(predictably porcine),
after an hour scrubbing
shit from under my nails.

I'd go mad, but I cannot
forget my name,
a dying fall
fat in their mouths.

Kiran Millwood Hargrave

My Garden

I know of a certain garden I'd like to take you to,
the winter stripped it bare, so I coloured it for you.
I first plucked out my eyeballs and then pulled out my teeth
to string up as a wind chime, for you to sit beneath.
The bunting is my bowels which I looped around and round,
my eviscerated stomach lies as poppies on the ground.
I put candles in my cranium, and hung it from a tree,
and thinly sliced my kidneys so they'd flutter in the breeze.
My spinal cord is ribbon, my arteries a bow,
I sliced across a major vein to decorate the snow.
I took a cutlet knife and carved your name into my lung,
and finished off with streamers made with slivers of my tongue.

For you I snipped along the lines and then peeled off my skin.
For you I opened up my chest, and let you see within.

Jodie Ashdown

Rhea's Revenge

You have made a litany of our lives,
husband, worthy of any myth. How
did they taste, I wonder? Each
small boy slipped down your gullet.
I trembled beneath your body as you sweated
out their sweetness, sweated in the next.

Take in enough water
to layer your pain,
you'll need it on your lungs
to stop the sounds.
Imagine each son
weighting your gut.

When I finally release, I'll haul you home
to prop against the hearth,
still wet from the sea. I'll cook samphire
in tight shoals of butter and lime,
and offer it to your conched mouth, massage
'til swallowed and watch your belly swell.

Later,
I'll cut you
groin to teeth
bury our children's bones,
the one black stone,
then feast.

Kiran Millwood Hargrave

Procne Prepares

I dream, for her, of the sour dust-salt of ship bedsheets
and spit chips of ground enamel into my bloody pillow.

I wake, for her, in brine water; drown in the wet air
and reek of roiling anger; gasp at the hot clutch of
want and hate that has me by the slipping tongue.

For her, I bruise and chafe my fingers, run them
bleeding over weft and warp: the what, where —
why. I cry for love that brought her to me

and so to him. Her hurts are mine and my
voice hers and, for her, I will fall to fly.

Here is the thrust and bone of it:

Fathered-eyed no-son of mine —
for her, I make a meal of you.

Slick stick of the knife then
mince, spice, simmer
for the count of a
lullaby sung
from me
to you,
for her.

Françoise Harvey

The Woman with No Name

Once more I wake and can't remember my name,
Mother veined to my underwear, stitched to my calves.

The sun frays his shirt I hold to my mangle all day,
knuckles falconry glove red, leathered by so much

laundering of love. I slip soap into my pocket, knot
a cloak to my neck like a stone and throw myself

into the snow. I march, boots ironing shovels of moon
into fields, breath rank, scraps of baby kisses stuck

in my teeth — tender rotten meat. The soap I rub foams.
I wonder who washes the soldier's clothes, salts out blood

stains, the shame out of cheeks. There's so much to mend.
The firelit mess window tatters night. Outside, I rub stars,

boy breath iced to the pane, nose pressed to heroes again.
Don't go in I warned him, I did. I can't take my own advice.

The hall smells of bread, a rise and fall of sleeping chests.
I lift up a sword, an arm, dropped toys on the floor. I hold

a cold hand, calluses on a palm mirror mine — our lives
knotted to our skin by the handle of a kindling axe. Drifting

bed to bed, stroke blonde skulls with a silver fingertip,
sleeping cocoons. Red Admirals fly, splash silk on my dress.

And I forget to etch a mother's name to each man's shield,
my own slips through my fist forgiving a latch on the door.

I walk, fingers uncurl, flakes fall, I leave freckles on the snow.

Angela Readman

In Beowulf, Grendel's mother is never given a name.

Salome's First Kiss

So I stood there, bells on my ankles still ringing
a toll of the second I had my stepfather's approval.
I caught his breath with a dance, I could dance. I was
more than a scrap of love caught in his wife's kiss
like leftover snack. Now, I could wow kings.
He asked what I wanted, I already had it, my mother
was a whole other matter. She whispered in my ear
soft as water finding a crack in a wall, seeping in.
I carried the head to my room before I gave her it.
I stared into the frozen fonts of its eyes, marrow
on the platter like jellyfish. Dints in the silver plate
wrestled the light, splashed waves on cold cheeks.
Everything rippled where the baptist's body should be.
I combed curls crusted to his hair, lay the plate on my bed.
There, on my silk sheet, he looked like a man in a river
swimming up to the surface, sprays of red sunlight
in his beard. He looked me in the eye, mouth open
for air, I kissed it and my childhood good night.

Angela Readman

PART 5

MYTH

Losing the Termagant

Maybe I'll let go of her in verse, the shrew,
her grab-ready hands and her pinched
chin, her volley of quick-picked
cavils, jabbed from needle-tongue.
Sleep-sparing, night-flying daybird,
I'll disembarrass her. Her face
always by mine, hair scraped
back, knitting-wool bound
round smallest thoughts. I'll loose her.

Like in a lucid dream, I'll imagine I'm gifted
to rinse myself in citronella
shake my shoulders and head
for the shore, river bed tilting
under my feet. I'll write that
I'll take a breath, whisper 'no' with my will,
coax heart to follow, me spilt and
spelling into blue-white-blue indelible.

Geraldine Clarkson

What goes of your father?
Surpanakha spits

So! Too forward, too loose,
full-mouth make-up, rusted hair,
bells and rings on all my toes, tattoo
too well-placed, too in your face,
double body, single clothes. What goes?
Tell! What goes of your father?

So, I am not one of these but maybe
one of those? My demon brother has ten heads
and twenty hands, but I am under no man's
thumb, out of control of fatherbrotheruncleson,
queening and loafing in my forest alone.
What goes, eh? What goes of your father?

So? Not pure, not demure, not shy,
I chose to be too much, too much myself,
out of bounds for you. Admit you liked it, no?
Unzipped your haloes? Your holiness slipped?
Brave heroes! Comecome! Cut off
my ears my nipples my nose. What goes?

So. Who is to judge, whose the sin?
I will change shape, grow myself back again.
Sharpen my wits to match my nails,
spit on my hands, slap my thighs.

Let the battle begin.

Imtiaz Dharker

Lilith's Love Song to the Monk

That fickle half moon
won't keep the darkness
from your room. You know

I'm waiting, birch-supple,
to unfurl from the shadows,
bud limbs from the dust.

Scratch another chalk line
with an unsteady hand.
It won't be enough.

Relentless as the sickle
I'll curve into your dreams.
Do those scars on your back

itch for my return?
Cold creeps inside sackcloth knees;
all your wicked heat

in those rosary beads.
Come, unveil me — the swell
of unbound hair like blood

screaming beneath the skin.
On your back please. Don't
expect me to submit like Eve.

I've howled the loss
of a thousand children. Sunset
after sunset I'll rise

to steal new seed.
Remorseless as stone,
my pale, demon flesh -

your hair-shirts are of no use
to me. I'll leave on pitiless wings,
refuse to dance with guilt

for your god. But you —
you'll twist, and burn, for this sin
with each sting of the flea.

Victoria Gatehouse

KASSANDRA #memoryandtrauma #livingilionstyle

Terribly terribly sorry (not) it's hard relating
to this one: you know, the dead wench in another country,
gifted but an attention-seeker? Your camera strikes
from afar. Like snakes licking out K.'s ears, men of power
seem caught up with her. More Twitter than other girls round her.
Your camera strikes. K.'s screwing up her eyes in a boat —
speaking for the sisterhood, but from that kind of family?
Why listen? She's privilege. Complication. Must be spoilt.
K.'s voice flares victim to her high-explosive hair; her thoughts
dismissable; cuntly, if you're a man; peripheral.

Take sixty seconds to re-read each of the lines above.
That took ten minutes: half as long as my death by stoning.

        Athena, grey-eyed, justicer,
        they've brought me back
        as if each stone
        broken for their roads
        and the rare earths
        mined for their devices
        vocalized my far-flung blood,
        but I have questions
        for you, law-giver, spoiler;
        also, plans to find
        which women you move
        in these greater days
        of privilege and complication.
        Holding on to you
        was the safe zone
        but the hero entered
        held and raped me
        in your precincts, justicer.

Why'd you let him do it? Why did you wait to strike him down?
Was it, in a way I do not understand, due process?

Does the burden of proof still fall on me, in modern courts?
As people encouraged by helpful foreigners to cross
a minefield may smile, stretchered, blinded or their legs blown off,
so each of my memories, a living and willing witness,
gets up to walk to you, to tell my story, but doesn't
make it. His camera strikes from afar. If you want it
to add up, why give me the gift of prophecy? I split,
spill truth like marrow from bones, gleaming on stone-strewn ground.

Vahni Capildeo

Guinevere, to All of Her Unborns

The river's tent is not broken, but bent
                        enough to leave you exposed,
            my sweets, clustered on the shore of my pulse,
the wet clutch of my muscle.

Why I can't bring you indoors:
                        I carry the gene that makes
            one susceptible to rain. There isn't enough
oxytocin to go round.

The dolorous stroke is wrenching
                        out a rib to make another
            And the wound that won't heal: women.
The story they keep telling:

that I am waiting to be sought.
                        That my men wander
            but I am lost in the cemetery where I went
one violet hour to sneak a cigarette

and startled a deer. A doe who darted
                        into traffic. Her fawn
            followed suit. River and current: one drags
the other along. Just as this land was never

my land: not my dust clouds rolling.
                        I hardly know my own mother
            tongue. They say the moon borrows its brilliance,
offers no light of its own. They say my river

runs soft, runs softly. Keep clinging to its bank,
                        my sweets. When I make my own map
            of the world, I'll sketch this shore, your pebbled
forms, in ochre and animal blood.

Shelley Puhak

Sionan and the Well of Wisdom

There is a tale the old ones tell,
that in the north you'll find a well
ringed all around with hazel trees
rimed with fruit and silver leaves.
And in the well a salmon swims
And eats the nuts and spins and spins
an endless knot of untold things,
until it bloats with rhymes unheard
except by those who fish for words.

She's heard the myth a thousand times
She knows the place, she's read the signs
Of desperate men who seek to know
that what's above is so below.
She thinks she too could catch a rhyme
and reel it in and have it shine
and rise above the role of muse
to wield her pen and write the rules.

But first the salmon must be caught
and all the knowledge, truth and art
that lies within its cage of bones
must be consumed and made her own.
But knowledge can be hard to grasp
and those who have it hold it fast.
From the well sprang seven streams:
inspiration, poetry, songs and dreams

rhymes and rituals, ancient lore
the water swelled and poured and bore
them all away downstream
and Sionan's screams
can still be heard on dark nights when words fail
and the world's wisdom seems to pale.

Sandra Ireland

Medusa

Days when I needed to slough my skin
stitch the wounds with fish bone twine
so I could suffer as I meant to; my statement
of intent. Days filled with stone, spent with only
me, days spent alone. Days I was a dissenter of my own

cause, days when I'd think to drop glasses
and shuffle across the floor on my hands and knees
just to bleed. Days spent watching the unravelling
and catching the threads just in time, stuffing the
secret into my head, fistfuls of hissing, black-eyed rot.

Days when I forgot. Days when I could not.
Days when days turned faster than a cricket
chirruping their victory on green legs that
I pulled off, clawed off until I caught the sun
and stared until my eyes were scarred with
daytime stars. Most days though, follow on.
It's a case of taking them, one by one.

Kiran Millwood Hargrave

Ophelia's Curse

enclave, i
the enormity of this morning
seeped between my pause, i found
drowning occurs when head hits ground
and blurs the sound of mourning, torn
between the paws of being born
and the jaws of being found — a warning
shot through the head of a wave

goodbye, this is not
the anointed verse
it is ointment for the fly,
Iscariot tongue greased with gaze,
and steeped in curse,
steeple, i
the vanishing point of
chariot and church.

Kalliope Amorphous

PART 6

RESURRECTION

Sixteen Winters

Mother, stone, hoarfrost —
each unsafe lune of the lost years
spent traipsing this wasted land,
cheerless, weather-bitten, musing

only on meeting noses, leaning
cheek-to-cheek with another
who lives to love me, swaddle
me in woman's flesh. Shivering

in febrile sleep, the same revolving
dream: a statue queen, winter flowers
at her feet, eyes, skin, cheeks all
warmed as she reaches out to touch

me; her treasure. My waking heart
dances, but not for joy, not joy —
alone in this garland, this mirror,
the world, pray who will hold me? Who?

Kaddy Benyon

A Dictionary of Mechanics, Memory, and Skin in the Voice of Marian Parker

The world is a wind I thought I heard just before
I heard nothing. The world is what the pulse of me
whispered just before it stalled. A lullaby
I drugged myself with while my slit throat emptied.

If I had risen the casual distance,
if I had run, if I had resisted like metal
not fired enough — but I can end if one man
asks it of me. Already my sewn eyes

are widows, delicate and desolate, a sabotage
in wails. Every direction in me is south. Every
sleep the deception of sleeping. Every corrosion
another part drought. I prefer to fail. I prefer

to be in pieces. No one expects from me now.
No mourning the model specimen, little Marian,
for what she was. The thin room of my animal's
whimper keeps night from the garden.

My limbs have their own dementia, decomposing
like a bloom. Fathers do not hesitate to collect
my rough bones. I will build a womb bathtub-cold
and be born, white as its porcelain, prone. I will

grow old in the minutes it takes to be dismembered:
one suture for each of my antiseptic mouths.
Tattered is how I began. It pleases me to rest among
the lilies though their bulbs long ago burned out.

Jennifer Militello

*Marian Parker was a 12-year-old child who was kidnapped,
murdered, and dismembered in 1927.*

A Letter to the Coroner in the Voice of Marian Parker

Lay me out as if the coffin is only a dress
or a wedding I never made it to. My God, I will
run off. My family will wait and I will be free
with my hair let down and I will not return.

I do not exist. I know where I belong.
I grow like roots to slow the going open,
to suffocate a moment's recent act,
removing the blood-like gloves it leaves.

Once inside me, the seasons go arid, the seasons
go mad, they complain of brambles. The crumble
of the mud earth sings, forms rot with a sweetness
breathing. Hours are our daily bread.

There is not a cartridge for all the darkness
I feel. My face is there, a molecule, a shiver
filled with June. I have clarity. I imagine
the shatter is a shatter that stays.

I am trying not to break. Debris is all I am.
My face gaunt where once it was seamless, entrails
replaced by rags, eyelids wired open, a congregation
in my eyes with all the candles held by children.

Come. The bleed of night
has an animal skin. There is livestock
in our hearts. How the dark sticks.
How the damp animal rakes before us.

Jennifer Militello

Lilith

I cannot die by heat or cold or blunt or sharp.
I cannot die in dark or light.
I cannot die starved. I cannot die gorged.
I cannot die bleeding, or pregnant, or hollow.
I cannot die by water.

I have cut a ribbon of skin from another man's body,
Dried it by the full moon and made a noose to bind you.
But you slide in knots like a bursting child
From the broken seas of birth.
I slide from knots.
I would break around your body.
In the blackness between red skies,
I would be the opening of your veins.
I would carry your blood in my mouth
And drown like the moon
And never leave the sky.

I have grown white with cold.
I have learned the lips of devils.
My kiss is cold.

Devon Miller-Duggan

Mary Magdalene gives an Exclusive Interview

***

Before him I was a disused rag cloth, an orphan.
Before him I was a fisherwoman with a rickety boat and fishing net.
Before him I was a woman with a hollow calabash for a womb
and I wanted my insides to bloom sweet fruit like coconut jelly.

***

The first time I see him I had just finished blowing conch
shell, to draw people to buy my daily catch.

***

I not ashamed to say that I stick on him like white on rice that morning
and ever since then I follow him through back roads and pastures.
Left all I had in the world to join his band:
One rickety fishing boat
One net full of fish
One old dry weather shack
One crocus bag hammock
One eighty-year granny
I hear nuff people fight over free fish that day.
I hear how Miss Nelly cook fish for two weeks straight.

***

My grandmother sap me up with Limacol
on headache nights, wash me out with castor oil,
Vicks cold out of my chest, rub tender
into my skin with coconut oil, but she never
tell me how woman could turn bazode over man,
follow man like fly drawn to sugar grain on tabletop.
How love could make you empty inside.
No she never prepare me for this.

***

I had a tabanka but I never told him,
I bury it in my foot bottom under the dry corn
on my big toe and never let it peep out.

***

I stand like marble under the cross, but you see when I left
there, I ripped up my dress and let go pure snot and eye-water.

***

Vex like hell — I shouted at them damn disciples:
why man like you, hard ears and stubborn like donkey so,
you all always want proof. How I go prove he live?
Look he here sitting in my nose hole!

***

I remember those nights we sat on a big stone
by the seashore, roasting fish in a coal pot.
Peter, Mark, Luke and John snoring like hog
And I would ask, *Master you go heal me if a fish bone
stick in mi throat and I drop dead?* How he would laugh
from the belly and say, *we go see when it happens
we go see. Cos if greed kill you, I can't save you.*

Malika Booker

Spare me that

Perhaps I shall not answer you truly in many things that you ask me, concerning the revelations; for perhaps you would constrain me to tell things I have sworn not to utter, and so I should be perjured, and you would not want that.
— Joan of Arc, 24 February 1431,
third public examination.

When your entire face tingles   *you are about to be tagged*

Domrémy-la-Pucelle's   cookbooks are still radioactive
story is   too dangerous to handle
held captive   by Le Pen

Finding a fire in your belly means   *you must comment*

Lead-lined for 400   years
you've been   costumed at every chance
whatever floats their boat   xenophobia or girl power
hive peg   into a square hole
cemented   in volumes

When no omens manifest   *you must sign in*

Ring the submerged   history

Paint   the walls with disembowelled voices
you   are multiple

Claire Trévien

The Death of Bonnie Parker's Right Leg

Would you believe while the battery
acid chewed through the back
of my thigh, I craved
                    lemon drops?
Strange how I remember

wood thrushes tapping amber
into the weeds; Clyde's voice howling
Baby, I'm so sorry. Sometimes
I want to slice off the tips
of his ears.

This was not one of those times.
Anyone else would run
if he saw a live tendon
sprawled out on his lap,
wheezing

its way back to bone.
He brings me morphine
for the ache. Bleach
for blood. Says I'll move faster
on his shoulder, anyhow.

This leg knows I'm too dumb to die
first. I can spell *Nacogdoches,*
                    bougainvillea,

but I'll let these muscles climb back
in like a clam's foot and live
out my hours in the backseat.
I'll hop out

to a dark fire, polish the barrels
and stocks. Swaddle salty hare in
                              apricot preserves.
My good knee shines,
                              a white biscuit,
and his eyes say to me things like:
No flour. No butter. My fault.

I ask him, *Don't you remember,*
Beloved, the unraveling bridge?
Was that not the sweetest
                              peppermint stripe
you'd ever wrapped your tongue around?

Meg Cowen

The Wife of Bafa

My name is Mrs Alice Ebi Bafa,
I come from Nigeria.
I'm very fine, isn't it?
My nex' birthday I'll be…twenty-nine.
I'm business woman.
Would you like to buy some cloth?
I've all de latest styles from Lagos,
Italian shoe an' handbag to match,
lace, linen an' Dutch wax.
I only buy de bes' an' I travel first class.
       Some say I have blood on my hans
'cause I like to paint my nails red
but others call me femme fatale.
My father had four wives
so I've had five husbands.
I cast a spell with my gap-tooth smile
an' my bottom power!
Three were good and two were bad.
       The first three were old and rich
an' I was young and fit.
They died of exhaustion!
The fourth one was ladies' man,
I could not count his women on one han'
but he'd rage if I looked at anoder man.
I was very wild when I was young.
They called me Miss Highlife,
I was not considered a good wife
but I always respected my husband.
He died when I returned from dis London.
       The fifth one I married for love.
He was studying law at University of Ibadon.
He was not yet twenty-one,
wicked in bed and so handsome
but he liked pornographic magazine.
His favourite was Playboy.
One day I threw it on fire
to teach him a lesson.
He turned into wife batterer.
He was to regret his action.
I beat him till he begged for his ancestors!

Now we get on like house on fire.
        Some say I'm a witchcraft
'cause I did not bear dem children.
They do not understand the Western medicine.
        You like my headtie? It's de latest fashion.
They sell like hot cake on Victoria Island.
Fifty pounds.
I give you discount 'cause I like your smile.
The quality is very good.
If I take off more I will not make profit
an' I travel to Lagos nex' week.
Make it my lucky day.
Please, I beg you!

Patience Agbabi

Angria

1.
Reader, I did not
marry him. & my sister Catherine
did not die; Lucy, our third, did not stand & wait.

Please, Bella Swan, stop dreaming
of us in our dead gowns & wan.
We haunt you when you make of us ghosts.

2.
At back of the North Wind,
a door. Fallen dolmen, high table
of the witches' sabbat, giantess' childbed.

We lifted it, Antoinette and I, on one secret flight
across the furze. Our rehearsals. I had read all
the bloody plays, knew the day would come: Choose.

Choose father, church and state, be kindly called.
Oh heavy stone. Stone in our mouth, stone
our hearts. We did not give in.

3.
The door under the hill
opens on stone. Flags, a passageway,
the scratch (needle, knife, pen). Our Fates,

wyrd mothers of neat and sharp, made us
in the compass of their lives. Snipsnip. We
didn't have much time.

4.
The door opens. That's what it's for. & we opened
it & opened until, in passing, we became ourselves
passage. Ghast, hag, bump in the: all the old

names they call us. Wuther. No matter. We are, we
are warning. We are your door: step through us,
furious, onto bare bracken, where the wind

in its raging
is our word
& yours.

Sophie Mayer

Poltergeistrix

First, she watches her lover's grief
with tasty horror. When he lies
face down and foghorns out her name,
she places her weightlessness along him,
sinks her fist into his chest
and rummages, touching the shuddering lungs
in turn, the heart chugging down
its jello-shots of blood.

She loves that she is presence
without mass: her pass says
access all areas and she does,
sampling all the things he'd not
be seen dead doing. Within a week,
she learns he likes his porn vanilla,
blonde and young; that when he comes
alone he wears a different face.

But without her, he's thuddingly dull.
After a month she's done
going bump in the night, writing
love notes in his minging human dust.
The pizza cartons piling up,
mugs scumming green and grey
til he runs out and buys a slub
of plastic party cups, the final straw.

It's been weeks now, but he's still
so lousy with the snot and tears
and stench of death, it's gross.
I want to see other ghosts, she says,
it's over — but he doesn't even flinch.
She spends a final night, fingering
things she'll miss: gilt picture frames,
a silver brooch, the cat. Not him.

By dawn, she's gone. Now being dead
is fun: she melts through buildings floor by floor
the way a good knife butchers wedding cake.
But the more she poltergeists around, the less
she's human: soon she's gawping through
their windows like this city is a massive,
boring zoo. They're all the same.
Dysfunctional, but ultimately dull as rust.

She gives up: finds a crypt whose lock is good.
There'll be no piss-stink, no kids crawling in
to smoke and fuck, just leaf mould
and the local dead. She's heard you get
a dying wish, and saved hers up,
but now she speaks it to the hunkered stumps,
the graveyard and its scary sky. Make sure
he never finds me. Better: never let him die.

Claire Askew

El Suicidio de Dorothy Hale

after Frida Kahlo

angel-armed clouds
cannot catch what falls
from the 33rd floor: you

who leapt, the wind flips
head first, diving, we wish
asphalt was water
but blood pools the frame
above which you lie
twenty rosebuds pinned to your black velvet gown

your nude-stockinged foot hangs
over the inscription, pointing
to your name: Dorothy, who stares
us down, Dorothy
holds out her hand, Dorothy
we see you fall

who saw you land

Amber West

Jonet Gothkirk to William Murdoch

*This was the thirteenth day of Jonet Gothkirk's publick appearance in Sackcloth
for her Adultery... because of her stupidity, and that she could discover no
sense or feeling for her sin, nor sorrow for ye same, she was ordained to
continue in ye place appointed for public Repentance —*
>   West Calder Kirk session minutes, 25 November 1677,
>   recorded on a placard underneath a sackcloth
>   down in the National Museum of Scotland.

I am Stupid in the same way
a treadle is duped into making
motion for the Machine,
Senseless as a shuttle, pass'd
betwixt and between Men
and their muscles, coil-sprung.

Oh, William of the last pew,
William of my roughest
wooing, what you weave
with those Fingers, nimble
and callus'd, threading through
one another, during my rebuke

from the pulpit, over, under —
my heart clatters! I know
Sorrow. That God so dour
crafted such a loom — those
Fingers, no smoother than
Sackcloth, but so fine, so long.

Shelley Puhak

Prayers from The Church on Marass Hill, Where The Clergy Waits for its Congregation

Mary crochets golden doves. Tinsel tidies
her bed preparing to bellow and gallop
meticulous she smoothes the sheets over
and over. Elia eases nylon onto her bare legs.
Lisa stares nocturnal again, and ready.
Cecelia sprinkles old prayers into the air,
for no raw pokes tonight, for gentle jasmine
bites tonight, for licks and sucks like soft breeze
tonight and the house to rock the hills tonight.
Prays, not to be breed up with no seeds
or disease tonight. Make these hills dance
ska tonight and let not petrol burn our valleys
tonight. Oh let our vendors jif be clean,
and seeds infertile tonight and make the breeze
sweet oh lord, so our deaths are like honey tonight.
So death no lick we down tonight.
So death no lick we down tonight.

Malika Booker

The Ridding

They take your lungs gut liver brain, peel out the
blood-rope twitch of every nerve and vein and they wed
you to his bed. Then they cut suck and lift the heart from
your eyeless pelt, with such hurt I mewled like a child. It
should be a mercy, but now my body's absence is solely
                        an echo chamber waiting for music.

I can remember nothing of your face or touch, no
voice or ways that you used to learn me, but I am full
of your songs. They rise through the jink of my ear
to the scoop of my sex until I am dizzy with melody
and can almost know the mouth upon the tune —
                        the pointed slip of tongue through teeth.

Tonight I dreamt I spilt dawn
into the webbed chambers of the underworld
with a look. The sun chased back the endless alchemy
of cold, and all the shrill shattering ways of ice
chattered into mouthfuls of water that I drank
                        cool and deep and perpetually.

How will I tempt another summer to seek me here,
in this well of embalming dark, kept hopeless in taxes
of a body's blood? My feet root in mimicry of the slow
ways of a seed — I plant myself on a thin scraping
of dusk, hoping for the break and spill —
                        the night's full extravagance of stars.

Kiran Millwood Hargrave

Purse

i.m. Emily Wilding Davison, suffragette 1872-1913

When I hold your purse in my hand —
to catalogue your archive
of school reports (glowing),
annotated minutes
militant with hope,
a Derby pass,
hate-mail hoping you die
more painfully than Anmer
(the King's felled horse)
and a flag folded against the grain
to show its bloodstain —
it fits in my palm like a paw.

      Film reel shows you fly
up from hooves like a scrap
of matter. Your purse is warm
as a thing just-caught.
When I roll its clasp undone
between index-finger and thumb
it's like stepping too sudden
from the kerb
into a traffic roar.

      I lay it in a perspex case
flanked by what it last held.
Your unused return.
An outbound, its torn edge
like fur under my finger.

Anna Kisby

The Purple, White and Green

In Rouen, God spoke to Joan of Arc.
In Shadwell, my vision is Christabel.
Dock-men yell, *Ain't she beautiful?*
as she tops a lorry to lecture, in violet silk.

Christabel catches in one sure hand a cabbage
fast-bowled at her throat. *I knew you'd lose
your head over me, old goat!* she calls, to howls.
I am lost in the rose of her vowels. Envisage

marching at her side, crying *Give women the vote!*
The bobby's hams for hands at my breast
where bruises spread. At Clement's Inn, Christabel
plans, at ease in Japanese slippers and kimono.

Covering my skin is a sheet pulled taut.
I lie on her bed like a sword.

Anna Kisby

*The colour scheme of the militant suffragettes, led by Emmeline and Christabel
Pankhurst, was purple for justice, white for purity and green for hope.*

Archives

You carry this one back in a Waitrose bag,
her mother's rosary pressed against
her warrant for arrest, head south
to the archive vault like crossing
the Styx. Each twist

        of the Northern Line
jostles a love letter closer
to her father. His stern moustache,
unwilling, tickles the words — *Eve, I shall
rig up a mosquito net for you under the stars —*

This is what keeps you awake: the dead
who all day long press upon you
wordy concerns, sepia stares begging
to be read. You smooth an obituary,
shelve two diaries

        close as palms in prayer. Ladies,
necks achy in over-ornamented hats, you slide
between acid-free sheets. Tonight
you will turn and turn again, and think:
it is her dust that I breathed in.

Anna Kisby

After Carolyn Steedman's writing on archive fever in
Dust: The Archive and Cultural History

Acknowledgements

Archives by Anna Kisby was published in *The New Writer*, 2011.

The Purple, White & Green by Anna Kisby was published in *Chroma*, 2009.

Nerrivik by Susan Richardson was first published *Where the Air is Rarefied* (Cinnamon Press, 2011).

The Pen is Mightier by Susan Richardson was previously published in *Ouroboros Review, issue 3*.

Jonet Gothkirk to William Murdoch and *Guinevere, to All of Her Unborns* by Shelley Puhak were first published in *Guinevere in Baltimore* (The Waywiser Press, 2013).

Lida and the Swan by Shelley Puhak was first published in *Stalin in Aruba* (Black Lawrence Press, 2009).

Wrecker by Emily Blewitt was first published in *Cheval* (Parthian, 2013).

A Daughter Sings from the Earth by Diana Brodie was previously published by *Kind of a Hurricane Press*.

Losing the Termagant by Geraldine Clarkson was first published by *Sentinel Literary Quarterly Anthology* (June 2012).

The Death of Bonnie Parker's Right Leg by Meg Cowen was first published by *The Pinch* (2012).

To sing as legends do by Nic Campeotto was first published in *The Mill*.

Medusa, Circe, and *Rhea's Revenge* by Kiran Millwood Hargrave first appeared in *wide-shining* (79 Rat Press, 2013) and *Splitfish* (Gatehouse Press, 2013).

Fishing, I Lose Another by Jenifer Browne Lawrence was first published in *Windfall* (Spring, 2008) under a different title.

The Wife of Bafa by Patience Agbabi is from *Transformatrix* (Canongate Books, 2000).

Greenham Common, 1985 by Julie-ann Rowell was published in *Angle* magazine, issue 5, 2014.

Warning by Malika Booker is an extract from *Pepper Seed* (Peepal Tree Press, 2013).

A Dictionary of Mechanics, Memory, and Skin in the Voice of Marian Parker by Jennifer Militello was published in *Los Angeles Review* (2010).

A Letter to the Coroner in the Voice of Marian Parker by Jennifer Militello was published in *The North American Review* (2013).

Biographies

Patience Agbabi is a sought-after poet, performer, mentor and Fellow in Creative Writing at Oxford Brookes University. She read English at Oxford and has an MA in Creative Writing from Sussex. She has lectured in Creative Writing at Greenwich, Cardiff and Kent Universities. Patience has spent over 20 years celebrating the written and spoken word. Active on the literature and arts scene, she's on the Council of Management for The Arvon Foundation. Her poem, *The Doll's House*, was shortlisted for the Forward Prize for Best Single Poem 2014. Her fourth collection of poems, *Telling Tales*, a contemporary version of *The Canterbury Tales*, was published by Canongate Books in 2014.

Kalliope Amorphous is an artist and poet best known for her work in creative self-portraiture. Much of Amorphous' work uses reflections, blur, mirrors, and multiple exposure to lead the viewer through the artist's favourite themes — identity, mortality, time, and consciousness. She currently divides her time between Providence, Rhode Island and New York City. www.kalliopeamorphous.com

Jodie Ashdown has just graduated from Cardiff Metropolitan University with a First class degree in English and Creative Writing, and has been accepted to the Masters programme to study an MA in Creative Writing. This is her first appearance in a major publication but she is active in the South Wales open mic scene, has had her writing featured in various local exhibitions and events, and is currently co-writing an audience-immersive play. She's an avid traveller, surfer, reader, writer and gin drinker.

Claire Askew's poetry has appeared in various publications including *The Guardian, Poetry Scotland, New Writing Scotland, The Edinburgh Review, The Feminist Wire, PANK* and *Popshot*. Her work has also won numerous accolades including the inaugural International Salt Prize for Poetry (2013), the Virginia Warbey Poetry Prize (2010) and a Scottish Book Trust New Writers Award (2012). Claire holds a PhD in Creative Writing and Contemporary Women's Poetry from the University of Edinburgh, and blogs at onenightstanzas.com

Kaddy Benyon was born in Cambridge and worked as a television scriptwriter for a number of years. Her poems have appeared in various literary magazines, on websites and in anthologies. In 2010 she was shortlisted for the inaugural Picador Poetry Prize with the manuscript for her debut collection, *Milk Fever* (Salt). In 2012 she was named a Granta New Poet and in 2013 she was highly commended in the Forward Prizes. She is currently Invited Poet at the Scott Polar Research Institute in Cambridge, where she is writing her second collection.

Emily Blewitt was born in Carmarthen in 1986. She has published poetry in *Cheval* (Parthian, 2012-2014), *Nu2: Memorable Firsts* (Parthian, 2011), and in *Brittle Star* (2011), and has work forthcoming in *Poetry Wales*. Her poetry appears online in *Pomegranate, Cadaverine, Bolts of Silk* and *The Guardian*. Emily won the 2010 Cadaverine/Unity Day Competition with her poem *Still Life,* and was selected as Honno's 'Poet of the Month' in September 2012. She has also appeared on BBC Radio 4's 'Lost Voices' programme to discuss the work of Anne Ridler. She is studying for a PhD in English Literature at Cardiff University.

Malika Booker is a British writer, poet and multi-disciplinary artist of Guyanese and Grenadian Parentage. She has represented British writing internationally, independently and with the British Council. Her first stage work, *Absolution,* was commissioned by The Austrian Cultural Institute and Apples & Snakes. Her poems are widely published in anthologies and her poetry collection *Pepper Seed* was published by Peepal Tree Press in 2013 and longlisted for the OCM Bocas 2014 prize. She was also the first British poet to be a fellow at Cave Canem, the prestigious African American poetry body. Malika was inaugural Poet in Residence at the Royal Shakespeare Company.

Diana Brodie is a New Zealander who has published widely in poetry journals and anthologies in the UK, USA, Austria and New Zealand. Her collection, *Giotto's Circle,* was published in 2013 by Poetry Salzburg.

Nic Campeotto is a genderqueer sometimes-girl who hails from the hotbox of Nashville, Tennessee, and has somehow found their way to Cleveland, Ohio, where they are currently studying Creative Writing and Gender Studies at Baldwin Wallace University. *To Sing As Legends Do* and several of their other poems have been published in Baldwin Wallace's literary journal, *The Mill,* for which they currently serve as Editor-in-Chief. Their hobbies include subverting gender norms, listening to egregious amounts of punk and shamelessly misquoting Lord Byron in an attempt to appear suave and charming.

Vahni Capildeo is a Trinidadian writer of poetry and prose. Her books include *Utter* (Peepal Tree, 2013) and *Measures of Expatriation* (Carcanet, due 2016). She has worked in academia, for the Oxford English Dictionary, and with Commonwealth Writers, and volunteered with Oxfam and the Oxford Sexual Abuse and Rape Crisis Centre. Her current project is translation-based.

Geraldine Clarkson's poems have appeared in *The Poetry Review, The Rialto, Poetry London, Tears in the Fence, Iota* and *Fuselit,* and she was the Selected Poet in *Magma 58*. She has read at various literary festivals and is working on her first collection.

Meg Cowen is the author of two chapbooks, *If Tigers Do Not Come* and *When Surrounded By Fire*. She has received the Elizabeth Curry Poetry Prize and is the founding editor of Pith (pithjournal.com). She writes, paints and lives in rural New Hampshire.

Imtiaz Dharker is a poet, artist and documentary film-maker. Her collections of poems include *Purdah* (Oxford University Press), *Postcards from god, I speak for the devil* and *The terrorist at my table* (all published by Penguin India and Bloodaxe Books UK), *Leaving Fingerprints* (Bloodaxe Books UK) and *Over the Moon* (Bloodaxe Books UK). Recipient of the Cholmondeley Award and a Fellow of the Royal Society of Literature, her poems are on the British AQA and Edexcel GCSE English syllabus, and she reads with other poets at Poetry Live! events all over the country to more than 25,000 students a year. She has had ten solo exhibitions of drawings in India, London, New York and Hong Kong. She scripts and directs films, many of them for non-government organisations in India, working in the area of shelter, education and health for women and children.

Jo Dixon is a graduate of the MA in Creative Writing at Nottingham University. Recently, she left teaching to embark on a practice-led PhD in poetry, funded by the AHRC. Her poems have been published in *New Walk Magazine* and *The Interpreter's House*.

Francine Elena has a chapbook of prose poetry, *Christmas Lantern*, published by 3:AM Press. Her poems have appeared or are forthcoming in *The Best British Poetry* 2013 (Salt), *Best Friends Forever* (Emma Press), *Par Avion* (3:AM Press) and the publications *Wasafiri, Clinic, Lighthouse 4, the Quietus, Poems in Which, 3:AM Magazine* and the *London Literary Project*. She has written about art, film and food for *Art Wednesday* and, recently, *The Guardian*.

Suzanna Fitzpatrick has been published in *Brittle Star, The Frogmore Papers, Fuselit, The Interpreter's House, HQ, Mslexia, The North, Poetry News, South,* and *South Bank Poetry*. She was awarded the 2014 Hamish Canham Prize, was commended in the 2013 Hippocrates Prize and the 2012 Poetry London and 2011 South Bank Poetry competitions, came second in the 2010 Buxton Competition, and has been shortlisted for the Bridport, Frogmore, and Keats-Shelley Prizes. She lives in London with her husband and young son.

Victoria Gatehouse was born in Leeds, originally trained as a Biochemist and has an MA in Poetry from Manchester Metropolitan University. Her poems have appeared in *Mslexia, Magma* and *The Rialto* and in several anthologies including *Not Only the Dark* for ShelterBox. In 2011 she won the Ilkley

Literature Festival Poetry Competition. Victoria has recently left full-time employment to spend more time with her children — and her writing.

Rebecca Goss grew up in Suffolk and returned to live in the county in 2013, after spending twenty years in Liverpool. Her first full-length collection *The Anatomy of Structures* was published by Flambard Press in 2010. Her second collection *Her Birth* (Carcanet/Northern House, 2013) was shortlisted for the 2013 Forward Prize for Best Collection and won the Poetry category in the 2013 East Anglian Book Awards. She blogs at rebecccagoss.wordpress.com.

Françoise Harvey grew up on the Isle of Man, though she now lives in London with her partner and two dogs. She writes poetry and short stories. She is one of three sisters, which might explain why she chose to write about the tragedy of Procne and Philomel.

Sandra Ireland is a postgraduate student at the University of Dundee, studying for an MLitt in Writing Practice and Study. To date, her work has been included in several poetry anthologies, in *Dundee Writes* and in *New Writing Dundee*. She also writes for women's magazines and her stories have been read out at the Byre Theatre, St Andrews, and at the Winter Words Festival, Pitlochry. Her paranormal novella, *Foxfire*, was published as an e-book in December 2012, and she is now working on a novel about the dark side of taxidermy. She lives in Carnoustie, Scotland, right beside the beach, which should be inspiring but is actually just very windswept!

Ailie Kerr lives in Plymouth, Devon with her family. She is seventeen years old and is currently in her last year of sixth form in Torquay. Next year, she will be a fresh(wo)man at Harvard University in Boston and intends to study either English or Folklore and Mythology. Writing is her chief love and she has assisted on residential creative writing courses for gifted students at Kilve Court in Somerset and was Plymouth's inaugural Young City Laureate last year.

Anna Kisby is an archivist and mother of three, living in Brighton. Her poems have been placed in competitions and published in a variety of magazines and anthologies, including *Magma*, *Mslexia*, the Pighog anthology *Skate* and *The Emma Press Anthology of Motherhood*. She was winner of the New Writer single poem prize 2011 and a finalist in Live Canon 2012.

Jenifer Browne Lawrence is the author of *One Hundred Steps from Shore*. Awards include the Orlando Poetry Prize, the James Hearst Poetry Prize and a Washington State Artist Trust GAP grant. Recent work appears in *Bellevue Literary Review*, *Los Angeles Review*, *Narrative*, *North American Review*, *Rattle*, and elsewhere. She is co-editor of the Seattle-based literary journal, *Crab Creek Review*.

Sophie Mayer is the co-editor of two award-winning feminist poetic activist projects: *Catechism: Poems for Pussy Riot* (English PEN, 2012), with Sarah Crewe and Mark Burnhope; and *Against Rape* (online via Peony Moon), with Michelle McGrane. She has recently co-edited *Glitter is a Gender* (Contraband, 2014) and co-written *signs of the sistership* (Knives, Forks and Spoons, 2013), both with Sarah Crewe. *(O)*, her third solo collection, will be published by Arc in 2015, followed by *kaolin* from Lark Books (US). She is currently completing a non-fiction book, *Political Animals: New Feminist Cinema* (IB Tauris, 2015).

Jennifer Militello is the author of *Body Thesaurus* (Tupelo Press, 2013; named a finalist for the Alice Fay di Castagnola Award by Marilyn Hacker), *Flinch of Song* (Tupelo Press, 2009; winner of the Tupelo Press First Book Award), and the chapbook *Anchor Chain, Open Sail*. Her poems have been published widely in such journals as *American Poetry Review, The Kenyon Review, The New Republic, The North American Review, The Paris Review*, and *Ploughshares*, and anthologised in *Best New Poets 2008*.

Devon Miller-Duggan has published poems in *Rattle, Shenandoah, Margie, Christianity and Literature, The Indiana Review, Harpur Palate*, and *The Hollins Critic*. She's won an Academy of American Poets Prize, two grants and a fellowship from the Delaware Division of the Arts, an editor's prize in *Margie*, honorable mention in *Rattle*. She teaches for the Department of English at the University of Delaware. Her first book, *Pinning the Bird to the Wall*, appeared from Tres Chicas Books in November 2008. Her chapbook of unsentimental poems about angels, *Neither Prayer, Nor Bird*, appeared from Finishing Line Press in September 2013.

Kiran Millwood Hargrave was born in London in 1990. She is a student on Oxford University's Creative Writing MA, President of the Oxford University Poetry Society, and a Barbican Young Poet. Her work has appeared in magazines such as *Agenda, Magma* and *Room*. She won the Yeovil International Literary Prize for Poetry 2013, and was shortlisted for the Cafe Writers' IS&T Poetry Commission 2013. Her latest collection is *Splitfish* (Gatehouse Press, 2013). Her debut novel *The Cartographer's Daughter* is forthcoming from Knopf, Random House in 2016.

Bridget Minamore is a writer from London. She has worked with the National Theatre's New Writers' programme, performed at the Southbank Centre, and has had poems exhibited at a TEDxLondon conference. She teaches poetry workshops and has a particular interest in working with and empowering teenagers and young women; she has spoken at three Inspirational Women Conferences for the Billericay School and has been involved in Plan UK's Day of the Girl campaign. Bridget has recently completed an English degree at University College London, been shortlisted to be London's first Young Poet Laureate, and blogs for arts organisation Poejazzi.

Helen Mort is the Derbyshire Poet Laureate. Her collection *Division Street* is published by Chatto & Windus and was shortlisted for the T.S. Eliot Prize and the Costa Prize. She has published two pamphlets with tall-lighthouse press, *the shape of every box* and *a pint for the ghost*, a Poetry Book Society Choice for Spring 2010. Fives-times winner of the Foyle Young Poets award, she received an Eric Gregory Award from The Society of Authors in 2007 and won the Manchester Young Writer Prize in 2008. In 2010, she became the youngest ever poet-in-residence at The Wordsworth Trust.

Shelley Puhak is the author of *Guinevere in Baltimore,* selected by Charles Simic for the 2012 Anthony Hecht Prize. Her first collection, *Stalin in Aruba,* was awarded the Towson Prize for Literature. She is also the author of the chapbook *The Consolation of Fairy Tales,* winner of Split Oak Press's Stephen Dunn Prize. Her poems have appeared in many journals, including *Alaska Quarterly Review, Beloit Poetry Journal, Kenyon Review Online, Missouri Review,* and *Ninth Letter;* and in anthologies such as *A Face to Meet the Faces: Contemporary Persona Poetry.*

Angela Readman's collection *Strip* was published by Salt. She has since won the Mslexia Poetry Competition, the Essex Poetry Prize and been commended in the Arvon International Poetry Competition, Cafe Writers, and the Cardiff International Poetry Competition. Her poems have appeared in journals including *Ambit, Staple, Bare Fiction, Magma,* and *Ink, Sweat & Tears.* She is also a twice shortlisted Costa Short Story Award winner. Her story collection *Don't Try This at Home* will be published by And Other Stories in 2015.

Susan Richardson is a Wales-based poet, performer and educator whose first collection of poetry, *Creatures of the Intertidal Zone* (Cinnamon Press), was inspired by her journey through Iceland, Greenland and Newfoundland in the footsteps of an intrepid eleventh century female Viking. *Where the Air is Rarefied* (Cinnamon Press), her latest collection, is a collaboration with visual artist Pat Gregory on environmental and mythological themes relating to the Arctic and sub-Arctic. Her new collection, *skindancing,* themed around human-animal metamorphosis, and exploring our dys/functional relationship with the wild, will be published in 2015. www.susanrichardsonwriter.co.uk

Isabel Rogers writes poetry, novels, short stories, flash fiction, sitcoms and sketches. She won the 2014 Cardiff International Poetry Competition. Her poetry has been published in various places including *Poetry Wales* and *Mslexia*, and was shortlisted in the recent Live Canon and Charles Causley competitions. She has just completed her second novel. She has lived in England all her life except for a decade in the Scottish Highlands.

Julie-ann Rowell started writing poetry while studying for her MA in Creative Writing at Bath Spa University. She won first prize in the New Writer Poetry Competition for a short collection, and was runner-up in the BT Section of the National Poetry competition in 2000. Her pamphlet, *Convergence* (Brodie Press), was granted a PBS Award, and her first full collection, *Letters North,* was nominated for the Michael Murphy Memorial Prize for best first collection in Britain and Ireland, 2011.

Elisabeth Sennitt Clough lives in the Netherlands with her husband and three children. She holds a Ph.D from the Open University. Her poems have appeared in UK poetry magazines and anthologies including *Other Poetry, Confingo* and the Cardiff Women's Aid Creative Writing Competition anthology. In 2013, she was shortlisted for the Bridport Prize. In no particular order, she is a fan of Simon Armitage, French food and builders' tea.

Claire Trévien is the author of *Low-Tide Lottery* (Salt) and *The Shipwrecked House* (Penned in the Margins), which was longlisted in the Guardian First Book Award in 2013. She edits *Sabotage Reviews, Verse Kraken,* and *Penning Perfumes.* clairetrevien.co.uk

Amber West is a feminist poet and theater-maker. Her poems have appeared in journals like *Calyx, The Feminist Wire,* and *Southword,* and in the anthology *Women Write Resistance.* Her plays and 'puppet poems' have been performed on the USA's east and west coasts. She has published essays in *Episodes from a History of Undoing: The Heritage of Female Subversiveness, The Routledge Companion to Puppetry & Material Performance,* and elsewhere. She earned her MFA at New York University and her PhD at University of Connecticut. She lives in NYC where she is director of the Puppets & Poets festival.

Rebecca White is a student at the University of East Anglia studying for a Masters in Creative Writing. She blogs at www.realrvwhite.wordpress.com and tweets from @realrvwhite.

Index of poets

For Books' Sake

For Books' Sake is the charitable organisation that centres, supports and champions writing by women and girls. Founded in 2010, For Books' Sake celebrates classic and contemporary writing by established, emerging and marginalised women authors through a national programme of live events, creative writing workshops, publishing imprint and other projects.

For Books' Sake aims to challenge and counteract systemic, institutionalised biases impacting women writers. The organisation provides an alternative platform and resources for writers, readers, publishers, educators and more, challenging inequality and empowering women and girls of all backgrounds and abilities to tell their stories and have their voices heard.

Previous For Books' Sake publications:
Short Stack: The Best New Pulp Fiction Written by Women (2012)
Derby Shorts: The Best New Fiction from the Roller Derby Track (2013)

Rape Crisis England & Wales

www.rapecrisis.org.uk

Rape Crisis England & Wales is an independent, registered charity providing essential support to rape crisis centres.

RCEW supports and promotes the work of its autonomous member Rape Crisis centres in England and Wales, and campaigns continuously to raise awareness of sexual violence, its prevalence and effects.

Rape Crisis centres provide crucial crisis and long-term specialised support, counselling and independent advocacy for women and girls of all ages who have experienced any form of sexual violence at any time in their lives; whether recently or in the past. Rape Crisis centres are community-based, and independent of government and the criminal justice system.

"As a feminist organisation, Rape Crisis England & Wales is delighted to be supported by an initiative that so powerfully tells women's stories, celebrates women's lives and herstories, amplifies women's voices and champions women's talent and creativity.

Our member Rape Crisis centres respond to over 150,000 helpline calls and provide ongoing specialist services to nearly 50,000 individual women and girls in England and Wales each year, and demand for this crucial work continues to grow.

Projects like *Furies* not only raise much-needed funds but also help us fulfill our aim of raising awareness and understanding of sexual violence, its prevalence and effects, so that the needs and rights of survivors can be more fully met and realised."

Eve Lacey was web editor for *Thresholds: Poets in Residence at the University of Cambridge Museums* before becoming poetry editor at For Books' Sake. In 2012, she was awarded the David Almond Fellowship from Newcastle University and Seven Stories Museum. She now works as a librarian and a longlist judge for the Commonwealth Writers Prize. Eve is also the editor of *The Emma Press Anthology of the Sea.*

Jenni Fagan is Writer in Residence at the University of Edinburgh, and was listed as one of Granta's Best of Young British Novelists in 2013. She has been shortlisted for The Desmond Elliott, James Tait Black and Dundee Book Prizes, as well as the Impac Dublin Literary Award. She won the 3:AM Poetry Book of the Year, was twice nominated for The Pushcart Prize, and has been described as 'the patron saint of literary street urchins' by The New York Times. Her début novel, *The Panopticon,* was published in 2012; her second novel, *The Sunlight Pilgrims,* is forthcoming in 2015.